Mastering The Mental Side Of Hitting

Hemispheric Kinesiology

Ernest Solivan

ISBN: 978-0-6151-7358-0

"Baseball is 90% mental. The other half is physical."
Yogi Berra

Table Of Contents

Table Of Contents

Introduction

With the advent of quantum physics, science must now acknowledge that there are things that happen below our level of conscious awareness that dramatically affect the experiences we create. The HK Hitting program is designed to work on a quantum level, or below your level of conscious awareness. That is where the blockages are preventing you from reaching your full potential to become a better hitter.

The first part of the book explains the development of Hemispheric Kinesiology (HK) and provides a foundational context on how your mind and brain influence the experiences (both positive and negative) you create on and off the baseball field. The second part explains how to use HK to become the kind of hitter you would like to become.

This is a book about HK and how you can use it to achieve peak performance in the batter's box. HK is a muscle testing technology that allows me to access, isolate and change undesirable subconsciously stored information preventing baseball players from achieving peak performance.

HK's most salient characteristic is that it offers a very credible, rational and viable explanation as to why you experience performance problems during competition and offers a remedy that will allow you minimize and/or eliminate those problems so that you may play to the best of your ability in the batter's box.

There is an old saying that you cannot teach an old dog new tricks. This is a testament to how difficult change is for just about everyone. There are basically three elements necessary to create change in your life. They are Sensation, Perception and Conception. Sensation is the capacity to experience; Perception is the capacity to be aware of what you are experiencing; and Conception is taking action to begin the process of change, or it can also represent a rebirthing into some new experience.

I refer to HK as "A Language Of Change" because it embodies all the elements necessary to facilitate and accelerate positive change in the athletes who experience it. HK does not diagnosis or label. Please respect the context in which I present this extraordinary and very effective discipline. It works on the simple premise that if it stresses you to step up to the plate for your turn at bat, you are not going to do it well.

Please set aside your prejudices, beliefs and judgments and do your best to keep an open mind. HK is a little different twist on psychology. This discipline was created with the intention of allowing you to help yourself facilitate and accelerate positive changes that will immeasurably improve the quality of your life on the baseball field, as well as in your personal life. And, isn't that what we are all looking for?

It is said that hitting is 95% mental and 5% physical. When you have finished reading Mastering The Mental Side Of Hitting you will understand why hitting is 100% mental.

The Mind

When you set a goal to do something, one of two things will happen. You will either succeed or fail. What determines your success or failure is the information contained in your Mind. This stored information is the information you will use while attempting to accomplish your goal.

If the information in your Mind supports you in successfully completing your goal, the accomplishment of your goal will be easy and almost effortless. However, if the information in your Mind does not support you in successfully accomplishing your goal, the accomplishment of your goal will be very difficult and require a tremendous amount of effort.

The Mind is generally thought to be the seat of consciousness. It is made up of every aspect of our being. There are many philosophies that view the Mind in a way that has created numerous fragments, i.e., the spiritual mind, the emotional mind, the etheric mind, etc. I found all these subdivisions of the Mind to be very confusing.

In HK I rely upon the very old axiomatic metaphysical concept known as "cause and effect." Several of the theories that support cause and effect are, "for every action there is an opposite and equal reaction;" "water seeks it own level" and "what goes around comes around."

Although I cannot see a player's Mind, I can see the experiences that Mind is creating. For instance, if I am working with a baseball player who cannot get his batting average higher than .190, I have to assume that he has information stored in his Mind to support him in hitting .190 or he would be doing something else.

It is important to note that your Mind supports you in everything you do. If you are failing, your Mind is supporting you in failing and it is doing so based upon information it has stored in its memory banks relating to success and failure. The player's physical body is merely acting out (i.e., can't get his batting average above .190) based upon this stored information, and it does it automatically.

To understand cause and effect, you must first understand that before anything physical happens in our lives, it must first start as a thought. So, if you want to change your undesirable experiences, you must change the thoughts that are responsible for creating those undesirable experiences.

For example, the information stored in the player's Mind is the cause while the experience he is creating (can't get his batting average above .190), or the acting out of his physical body is the effect. The effect, which this player is creating in his reality is clearly an undesirable effect, and he has no idea how to change it.

The information he is using is causing him to sabotage his success. The goal of HK is to change the information in this player's Mind, and to do it as quickly as possible. Once he accomplishes that, his experience will change. When you change your thinking, you will change the experiences you are creating with those thoughts.

Before I explain how this is accomplished, it is important to establish a context and foundation whereby all the contributing factors to this failure phenomenon may be examined and understood. It is noteworthy to point out that in HK, all we are dealing with is information. For instance, although an emotion is something we can feel, it is stored in the Mind as information.

The Mind has basically two parts. The Conscious Mind, and the Subconscious Mind.

The Conscious Mind

The Conscious Mind is known as the "knower" because it has the ability to be aware of itself. It has the capacity to be aware of what it is thinking and feeling in the normal waking state. It also has the ability to know what it is doing and why. One of the major functions of the Conscious Mind is its use of volition. Webster's defines volition as, "the act of using the will; exercise of the will as in deciding what to do; a conscious or deliberate decision of a choice thus made."

You are where you are in your life right now as a direct result of the choices you have made using the volitional part of your Conscious Mind. The Conscious Mind provides us with short-term memory and can only focus on one thing at a time. The Conscious Mind uses the five senses; sight, hearing, smell, taste and touch, to collect information which allows it to experience awareness.

The Conscious Mind uses this collected information to formulate your self-image, your prejudices, and your belief system. The most important function of the Conscious Mind is that it allows us to set goals. The information collected by the Conscious Mind will influence the formulation and successful completion of the goals we set throughout our lives.

So, what happens when the Conscious Mind, using its volition, decides to engage in some particular activity? Well, it types out a memo of the instructions and sends it to the Subconscious Mind.

The Subconscious Mind

When you engage in a particular activity, like hitting, it is the responsibility of your Conscious Mind to decide the nature of the activity. Your Conscious Mind will send instructions to your Subconscious Mind, "Send me all the information you have relating to hitting." If the information accessed from your Subconscious Mind is supportive, you will perform the activity easily and efficiently. However, if the information accessed from your Subconscious Mind is not supportive or contradicts the goal set by your Conscious Mind, your activity will become very difficult and require a tremendous amount of effort.

The Subconscious Mind is a part of the Mind known as the "doer" because it merely does what it is programmed to do. Unlike the Conscious Mind, the Subconscious Mind does not have the capacity to exercise volition, it merely "does." The Subconscious Mind acts out thorough the physical body and uses information it has stored in its memory banks relating to the particular activity. This "acting out" is done instantaneously and automatically. The information arrives into the Subconscious Mind through the Conscious Mind using the five senses (sight, hearing, smell, taste, and touch).

The Subconscious Mind is a storage facility for all information that enters through the Conscious Mind. The one important feature to note about the Subconscious Mind is that when it is storing information it is impersonal. It doesn't say, "I am not going to store this experience because it was a bad experience." IT STORES EVERYTHING! The Subconscious Mind also provides us with long-term memory, and is the receptacle for our belief system.

The Subconscious Mind does not have a sense of humor. It cannot tell the difference between a joke and something serious. Additionally, the Subconscious Mind cannot distinguish between something real or imagined.

The Subconscious Mind can be likened to the hard drive of your computer with one notable exception. When using a computer, you have the option of saving or erasing the information on your screen. Every piece of information that enters the Subconscious Mind is stored. Your Conscious Mind will eventually use this subconsciously stored information when it engages in an activity that corresponds to the information in storage. The Subconscious Mind will provide the Conscious Mind with whatever information is has available. This information can be supportive as well as non-supportive information.

If there is one thing I would like you to get from reading this book it's that everything we do is subconscious. Do you remember years ago as a child when you were first learning to tie your shoes? At first it took a tremendous amount of time and effort. Now, you do it without thinking because it has become a subconscious act.

That is exactly what is happening with every other aspect of your life. When you are standing in the batter's box you don't stop and ask yourself "What do I do now?" Everything is moving too quickly for your Conscious Mind to get involved and you are at the mercy of the information stored in your Subconscious Mind and it will dramatically influence how you perform that day. That is, your physical body will "act out" based on whatever information is stored in your

Subconscious Mind.

There is a very integral component of the Mind that gets involved when the Conscious and the Subconscious Mind interact. It is known to as the Critical Factor.

The Critical Factor

After information enters the Conscious Mind, it is reviewed prior to storage in the Subconscious Mind. The responsibility for this task belongs to a component of the Mind known as the Critical Factor. The Critical Factor literally criticizes or reviews information that comes into conscious awareness. After its review, the Critical Factor must make a decision regarding the disposition of the information. The Critical Factor has two options. It can either store the information, or reject it.

Everyone knows that the color of the sky is blue, but suppose I told you that the color of the sky was red. When that statement enters your Conscious Mind, your Critical Factor will stop it momentarily and says something to the effect, "Let me check the information I have in subconscious storage relating to the color of the sky." The Critical Factor checks and discovers that the information stored in the Subconscious Mind indicates that the color of the sky is blue. The Critical Factor proceeds to reject the statement, "The sky is red."

Getting back to the player who could not get his batting average above .190, his Critical Factor could not allow him to hit higher than .190 because the information stored in his Subconscious Mind contradicted the intentions of his Conscious Mind. Whenever this player got close to hitting more than .190, his physical body would created so much stress that his swing would totally fall apart. It's as if the Critical Factor goes on "red alert" and, using the player's physical body, proceeds to sabotage his visits to the plate.

Imagine the Critical Factor as a guard, and that it is guarding all information coming into and leaving your

Mind. How do we change this information? How do we change subconsciously stored information causing us to exhibit undesirable behavior patterns, or causing us to create undesirable experiences in our lives? In order to change subconsciously stored information, we must achieve Critical Factor Bypass.

Critical Factor Bypass

Critical Factor Bypass occurs when new information is allowed to bypass the Critical Factor of the Mind in an effort to change old information stored in the Subconscious Mind. HK can achieve Critical Factor Bypass, which enables you to literally change subconsciously stored information. Using HK to achieve Critical Factor Bypass allows us to accelerate change for the players who experience it. In order to more fully understand Critical Factor Bypass, we must first look to the advertising industry.

On many occasions advertising agencies will send sales copy to a psychologist, and ask, "Will this copy achieve Critical Factor Bypass for our product?" The ad agencies know that if they can achieve Critical Factor Bypass on anyone who hears or sees their commercials, their chances of selling their product or service are greatly enhanced. They carefully choose the people who star in these commercials, carefully choose the wording, and carefully choose the scenarios.

How can they motivate someone to buy their product or service? One way to do it is using fear in the form of authority figures. It cannot be done blatantly. It must be subtle. Have you ever noticed that in many commercials, ad agencies will use policemen, judges, doctors, or firemen. All these professions represent authority figures and the ad agencies know that when a policeman tells you to do something, you normally do it without question. You do what you are told because the policeman was able to achieve Critical Factor Bypass.

Another very subtle tactic ad agencies will use to create Critical Factor Bypass is race and gender. I once saw a print ad that contained a Caucasian, an

African-American, an Asian, an older gentleman, an older woman, a young man, and a young woman. They covered a lot of bases with that ad.

Sometimes the ad agencies will appeal to your emotions. I am certain you have seen the Michelin Tire commercial with a baby sitting in a tire. That commercial has been running for years. This particular commercial has been successful because the ad agency was able to achieve Critical Factor Bypass by using the baby to appeal to the emotions of the viewer. Michelin must be selling a lot of tires, or they would not continue to use this very effective commercial.

Some of the other tactics used by ad agencies are humor and money. For instance, sometimes the thought of saving money will compel someone to purchase something they don't even need. In fact, the next time you view or hear a commercial advertisement, ask yourself, "What are they doing in this commercial to achieve Critical Factor Bypass?"

I will explain in a subsequent chapter how we are able to achieve Critical Factor Bypass using HK. We have, up to this point, examined the nuances of the Mind to include the Conscious Mind, the Subconscious Mind, the Critical Factor, and Critical Factor Bypass. The Mind must act out through the physical body and it does this using the brain.

The Brain

Although the Mind is the decision maker, it is the brain's responsibility to carry out those instructions. The brain is a part of the Central Nervous System composed of approximately 10 billion nerve cells. Each cell is linked to one another, and together they are responsible for the control of all functions in the physical body. The brain disseminates these instructions throughout the physical body using information provided by the Mind in the form of electrical impulses.

As I had mentioned earlier, working with the Mind is so challenging because we cannot see it. Although we cannot see a player's Mind, we can ascertain facts by observing what kinds of experiences that player's Mind is creating. If, for example, someone with whom I am working is creating struggle at the plate, I have to assume that there is information stored in his Mind to support him in struggling, or he would be doing something else.

`The brain is an organ consisting of three major components. The Left Hemisphere, The Right Hemisphere and the Corpus Callosum. Although these three components are integral, they each have very specific and different functions, and can function independently should the need arise. The Left Hemisphere of the brain controls the right side of the physical body, while the Right Hemisphere controls the left side.

We need only look at a stroke victim to understand this phenomenon. Notice that in the majority of the cases only one side of the body is paralyzed. That's because the hemisphere of the brain on the opposite side of the affected area was so severely damaged during the stroke that it manifested as paralysis. The corresponding side of the physical body is not receiving electrical impulses (information) from the damaged hemisphere resulting in partial or total paralysis. There are degrees of dysfunction between the brain and the physical body, and that total paralysis represents the extreme.

Since the Left and Right Hemispheres of the brain can function independently and have their own responsibilities, they need some way to communicate. This is accomplished using the Corpus Callosum. The Corpus Callosum is a band of nerve fibers that connect the Left and Right Hemispheres of the brain. The hemispheres share and exchange information (electrical impulses) that will eventually be disseminated to the physical body.

What I realized in my research in working with athletes over the years was that the hemispheres of the brain have a tendency to weaken or switch off. When one hemisphere is switched off, the opposite hemisphere will dominate. For instance, if a your Left Hemisphere is switched off, your Right Hemisphere will dominate whatever activity you may be involved in, and vice versa. The hemispheres of the brain are continually influenced by and are reacting to stimuli in an individual's immediate external environment.

An excellent case in point occurred when I had worked with the Arizona State University men's golf team in 1991. The director of the golf program was observing one of the sessions with one of the team members on the driving range. He commented that the player was muscle testing weak for everything, as all the statements were relating to golf.

So I turned to the young man and asked him what his favorite school subject was. "Math," he replied. I then asked him to imagine himself doing Math. The young man muscle tested strong, and both hemispheres of his brain were strong or switched on. Then I asked him to imagine himself playing in a collegiate golf tournament. The young man muscle tested weak, and both hemispheres of his brain were weak or switched off.

When he was doing Math, his physical body was relaxed, and both hemispheres of his brain were strong or switched on. The information he was accessing from his Subconscious Mind relating to Math supported him in doing it well and he excelled. However, when he stepped on the golf course, it immediately created stress in his physical body, which weakened or switched off both hemispheres of his brain. Whatever he did on the golf course was a struggle. By the way, this player won his first collegiate golf tournament within thirty days after our session.

The brain does basically three things. It processes (learns), stores, and disseminates information. What kind of information? That would be any and all information relating to pictures, sounds, fragrances, culinary data, and touch. All three of the major components of the brain come into play when the brain is exercising these functions. Let's first examine the Left Hemisphere of the brain.

The Left Hemisphere

When the Left Hemisphere of the brain processes (learns) information, it only understands words, language and numbers. That's because the Left Hemisphere processes information sequentially, or one piece at a time. The Left Hemisphere is one-dimensional, and can only focus on one thing at a time. The Left Hemisphere controls the right side of the physical body and it accomplishes this by sending information in the form of electrical impulses.

When the Left Hemisphere of the brain weakens or switches off, during the processing or learning stage, it's as if a short circuit occurs in the electrical field in the physical body, and the incoming information never reaches the hemisphere of the brain that is switched off.

Incoming information will only store in the hemisphere that is switched on. For instance, if your Right Hemisphere is switched off while your brain is learning, the incoming information will store in your Left Hemisphere. Now, because there was no information stored in your Right Hemisphere, when it's time for your brain to disseminate the information to you at some point in the future, you will only receive information from your Left Hemisphere. It's as if you are only getting half the information.

When the Left Hemisphere of the brain stores information, it will only store sequential information such as words, language and numbers. It will store information that is logical and organized. In other words, the information stored in the Left Hemisphere must be structured.

When the brain disseminates information to the physical body, the Left and Right Hemispheres deal with different and specific information. The Left Hemisphere of the brain provides the physical body with the following information and attributes:

Logic, action, decision making, critical, one-dimensional, mechanical, compulsive, doubt, cautious, judgmental, hardworking, action, limitation, shame, rational, stoic, organization, reasoning, specificity, structure, boundaries, rules, rigidity, opinionated, intense, impersonal, cold, unfeeling, introverted, controlled, predictable, restricted, precise, serious, conservative, quiet, hard, intolerant, scientific, temporal (the now) arrogant, fearful and finite.

When you engage in an activity and the Right Hemisphere of your brain is weak or switched off, your physical body is only receiving information, or a majority of the information, from your Left Hemisphere. This causes you to become left-brain dominant while you are engaged in that particular activity. The result is that you will exhibit one or more of the personality traits listed above.

For example, a left-brain dominant individual is introverted, dresses very conservatively, and is very structured. When we access information from only one hemisphere of the brain, it's as if we are only receiving half the information available to us. This phenomenon can create very dysfunctional experiences for the left-brain dominate individual.

Since our thoughts create our experiences, you can clearly see that many of us are only using half of the information available to us. Where is the other half of this information located? It is located in the Right Hemisphere of the brain.

The Right Hemisphere

When the Right Hemisphere of the brain processes information, it only understands movement and pictures. That's because the Right Hemisphere is spatial and can process information collectively rather than sequentially. This collectiveness allows it to process large amounts of information at one time. It can only process information that has no structure.

For instance, if you were looking at a picture of a landscape with your Left Hemisphere, you would have to look at every piece of the picture individually because the Left Hemisphere processes information sequentially. You cannot see the whole picture if you are only looking at one piece. The collective capabilities of the Right Hemisphere allows you to see the whole picture, while the Left Hemisphere provides you with the capacity to structure the collective information in the form of discernible images.

When we examine this phenomenon during the learning stage of our development, we can clearly see how the hemispheres of the brain influence how we learn. Let's look at an elementary school student named Harold. He is learning to read the sentence, "See Jack jump." If Harold had the Right Hemisphere of his brain weak or switched off while reading this sentence, his Left Hemisphere would dominate.

Now, keeping in mind that the Left Hemisphere processes information sequentially, Harold's Left Hemisphere will know and understand the words <u>see</u>, <u>Jack</u>, and <u>jump</u>. However, because Harold's Right Hemisphere is weak or switched off, Harold will have difficulty achieving total comprehension. In order for that to happen, he would have to send the information from his Left Hemisphere, via the corpus callosum, to the Right Hemisphere, and request additional information such as a visual of a boy jumping. With both hemispheres of his brain participating in the learning process, Harold will achieve total comprehension, no matter what he is learning.

When the brain disseminates information to the physical body, the Right and Left Hemispheres deal with different and specific information. The Right Hemisphere of the brain provides the physical body with the following information and attributes:

Feelings, emotions, relaxation, beliefs, creativity, flexibility, physical movement, tolerance, visualization, artistic, spatial, self-esteem, forgiveness, no boundaries, unstructured, generalizations, procrastination, compassion, optimism, funny, passive, unreasonable, loud, expressive, foolish, passionate, charming, humility, intuition, love, uncontrollable, multi-dimensional, imagination, addictions, lazy, laid back, open-minded, unorganized and infinite.

When the Left Hemisphere of your brain is weak or switched off, the Right Hemisphere will dominate your activities, from your decision making to your personality. Since your physical body is only receiving information from the Right Hemisphere of your brain, you will exhibit one or more of the above listed personality traits and attributes. Think of the many times that a particular event in your life has saddened you, or the many times you were very passionate about a particular cause. It is during these times when the Right Hemisphere of your brain was dominating your thinking.

The objective in HK is to switch on both hemispheres of your brain in relationship to a thought, statement or action. Having both hemispheres of your brain switched on insures that you will have access to information such as judgment, analysis and structure (Left Hemisphere), as well as creativity, imagination and intuition (Right Hemisphere). With both hemispheres of your brain providing your physical body with information, you will experience total balance in your life, no matter what the activity.

A great analogy for explaining hemispheric balance is water. The Right Hemisphere can be likened to boiling hot water, while the Left Hemisphere is ice-cold water. By themselves, their temperatures are very uncomfortable. However, when you mix them together, you get a warm, comfortable and balanced temperature. When both hemispheres of your brain are switched on, you enter a mental space that athletes refer to as "The Zone."

Another salient difference between the hemispheres worthy of note is that the Left Hemisphere deals with "old" information, while the Right Hemisphere deals with "new" information. I once did a session with a player before a game in which his goal was to hit .350 during the game. When I checked his hemispheres using muscle testing, his Right Hemisphere was weak or switched off, while his Left Hemisphere was strong or switched on.

The results from the muscle testing told me he was approaching the goal of hitting .350 with his Left Hemisphere and that he was using old information. In other words, he was thinking "What did I do last week to hit .350, what did I do last month to hit .350;

Etc." Without the creativity provided by the Right Hemisphere of his brain, he will continue to use the old information creating the same result.

This may explain why some people seem to make the same mistakes over and over, or repeat the same behavior patterns throughout their lives in spite of their efforts to change. When you are in your Left Hemisphere, you will continue to use old information even though it didn't work last week or last month. Without the new information provided by the Right Hemisphere in the form of creativity, it's as if you are walking through a mental revolving door. This new information augments and integrates with the old information allowing you to constructively handle whatever challenges you may be encountering at that moment.

There is another excellent analogy to contrast the hemispheres of the brain, and how they handle specific tasks. Let's assume that you have just purchased something that requires assembly. The Left Hemisphere of your brain will approach the task by saying something like, "Where are the instructions to this thing (?); I can't put this together without the directions!" Remember that because the Left Hemisphere is using old information, it is basically asking, "Show me the way some else did it, then I can do it."

Conversely, the Right Hemisphere will approach that same task by saying, "Hey, even if we don't have the instructions, let's put it together anyway." That's because the Right Hemisphere is providing the physical body with new information in the form of creativity, and will figure it out eventually. The Right Hemisphere will risk (no instructions), while the Left

Hemisphere will tend to play it safe (must have instructions).

When you can function at the plate with both hemispheres of your brain strong or switched on, your batting average will go through the roof. With access to structure, judgment and organization (Left Hemisphere), and creativity, intuition and imagination (Right Hemisphere), every decision you make at the plate supports you in being more productive during your at bats. HK helps you clear the blockages preventing you from realizing your true potential to become a premier hitter.

In HK it is imperative that we know what activity is taking place in the physical body in relationship to a statement, thought or action. This is accomplished using Muscle Testing.

Muscle Testing

There are three vital pieces of information necessary in HK in relationship to the subject matter which muscle testing allows me to obtain in relationship to a statement, thought or action. First, muscle testing allows me to determine whether the physical body is weak or strong. Secondly, muscle testing allows me to determine the condition of the hemispheres of the brain. Thirdly, muscle testing allows me to post test and validate that the stress has been cleared from the physical body.

Muscle testing is a technique that has been widely used in the alternative health field for years and has been used in a variety of applications. I use muscle testing to determine whether stress is present in a player's physical body relating to a statement, thought or action. Since the physical body is merely acting out based upon information contained in your Subconscious Mind, muscle testing allows me to tap into that subconsciously stored information.

In his book "Switching On," Dr. Paul Dennison defines muscle testing as:

> "Muscle testing is the art of isolating and testing one muscle at a time in order to determine if it is 'weak' or 'strong', relative to the strength of the individual being tested."

There are forty-two muscle groups in the physical body. In HK, I muscle test the deltoid muscle. The deltoid is the larger triangular muscle of the shoulder, which raises the arm away from the side. If you held your right arm straight out from your side, parallel to the ground, and lifted your arm upward from that point, it is the deltoid muscle that allows you to execute that movement.

When I muscle test someone I will ask them to:

1. Stand with weight evenly distributed on both feet;
2. I have the subject hold his left or right arm straight out or parallel to the ground;
3. I face the subject standing in front of the outstretched arm;
4. I ask the subject to look straight ahead and extend the fingers of his outstretched arm so that they are parallel to the ground;
5. I place my left hand on the subject's left shoulder for support;
6. I place my right hand, using only two fingers (index and middle fingers) on top of the subject's outstretched arm between the elbow and wrist;
7. The subject is now ready to be muscle tested;
8. I will ask the subject to resist upwards slightly, towards the sky, while I apply about 2 ounces of pressure downward towards the ground. This allows both the subject and I to get a feel for the muscle test.

The key to muscle testing effectively is 2-2-2. Use two fingers, apply two ounces of pressure, and hold for two seconds. There are two possible responses to a muscle test. Strong, or weak.

A strong muscle test indicates that my downward pressing motion was unable to budge the subject's arm. A strong muscle test also indicates that there was no stress present in the subject's physical body relating the statement, thought or action for which I muscle tested. A weak muscle test indicates that the subject was unable to resist my downward pressure, and could not hold his arm parallel to the ground. A weak muscle test is evidence that stress was present in the subject's physical body relating to the statement, thought or action for which we muscle tested.

What does a strong vs a weak muscle test tell me, if anything? Well, if I had had you make the statement, "I am a .400 hitter," the strong muscle test signifies that your physical body would totally support you in becoming a 400 hitter. The absence of stress in your physical body indicates that there is information stored in your Subconscious Mind that would support you in becoming a .400 hitter, and you will do it well.

On the other hand, had you muscle tested weak to the statement relating to hitting .400, the weak muscle test indicates the presence of stress in your physical body relating to the statement. It basically stressed you to say, "I am a .400 hitter." The weak muscle test tells me that the information stored in your Subconscious Mind would not support you in hitting .400.

A weak muscle test is the physical body's way of saying, "I am not doing that because I do not have information stored in my memory banks to support you, or that the information I have stored contradicts whatever it is you want to do."

The second piece of information I can obtain using muscle testing is the condition of the Right or Left Hemispheres of your brain in relationship to a statement, thought or action. For instance, when checking the condition of the Left Hemisphere, I merely touch the left side of your head and muscle test. If I record a strong muscle test, the hemisphere is switched on. If I record a weak muscle test, the Left

Hemisphere is switched off. I would do likewise to check the condition of the Right Hemisphere.

Checking the hemispheres of the brain allows me to determine how you would function while engaged in the activity for which we are muscle testing.

Thirdly, and most importantly, muscle testing allows me to validate, through post testing, that the stress relating to the subject matter has been cleared from your physical body. If I have you state "I am a .400 hitter," and you muscle test weak, and then have you say it again, and you muscle test strong, something obviously changed in your physical body and the way it reacted to the statement.

In HK, muscle testing allows me access to your Subconscious Mind. If subconsciously stored information is to be changed, it must be done subconsciously. Muscle testing allows me to inferentially (indirectly) access information from your Subconscious Mind using your physical body. That's because the Mind and the physical body are integral and mirror each other. What affects the Mind equally affects the physical body.

When the physical body is in a weakened state, it is engaged in a phenomenon known as sabotage. Muscle testing allows me to interpret the language used by the physical body to communicate this sabotage state, and that language is Stress.

Stress

WHENEVER THERE IS CONFLICT BETWEEN THE CONSCIOUS AND SUBCONSCIOUS MIND IT WILL ALWAYS MANIFEST IN THE PHYSICAL BODY AS STRESS!

It's as if the Conscious Mind and the Subconscious Mind are not on the same page. When stress is present in the physical body, it will always result in a weak muscle test and cause one or both hemispheres of the brain to weaken or switch off. The presence of stress creates a short circuit in the electrical system of the physical body and causes a biological fuse to blow.

It is crucial that you understand this phenomenon because it is at this juncture in the failure process that your physical body begins to sabotage your visits to the plate. When the physical body is in this stressed state, it goes on red alert because the information in the Conscious Mind does not match the information accessed from the Subconscious Mind. The Subconscious Mind acting out through the physical body will do everything in its power to sabotage your success.

Taber's Cyclopedic Medical Dictionary defines stress as, "…the result produced when a structure, system or organism is acted upon by forces that disrupt equilibrium or produce strain…the term denotes the physical and psychological forces that are experienced by individuals." Stress has an absolutely pervasive effect on the physical body, and the prolonged presence of stress in the body can manifest pathologically (disease).

When stress is present in the physical body, it creates a myriad of physiological changes. Some of the more salient physical reactions to stress are:

* Increase in the rate and force of heart beat;
* A rise in systolic blood pressure;
* Sweating of the palms and hands;
* Dilation of the pupils;
* Decreased digestion;
* Blood distribution from less to more active organs;
* Increased blood glucose (hyperglycemia);
* Etc.

Imagine trying to bring in the winning run during the bottom of the 9th with all this activity going on in your body. When stress is present in the physical body, it interrupts the electrical signals from the brain to the muscles causing the body to weaken. It is when the body is in this weakened state that the sabotaging phenomenon occurs. You will either get called out on strikes or swing at a bad pitch.

This sabotaging phenomenon is so subtle that you will be totally unaware that you are doing it because it is all happening subjectively or subconsciously. That is to say that it is happening below your level of conscious awareness. All athletic movement, including swinging a bat is subconscious in nature.

Swinging a bat at a 95 mph fastball occurs in a matter of seconds. Remember that earlier we stated that one of the limitations imposed upon the Conscious Mind is that it can only focus on one thing at a time. The swing of the bat is occurring too quickly for the Conscious Mind to become involved. Therefore, the physical body is relying totally on the information contained in the Subconscious Mind in order to properly execute the movement.

It is important to note that there are different levels and degrees of stress that may manifest in the physical body ranging from very subtle to very severe. When a player swings at a pitch it is impossible to see stress in his body with the naked eye.

However, since his Subconscious Mind stored that information, I can access that information later by merely asking him to remember the swing and a miss that resulted in his striking out during the 3rd inning. I can then muscle test to determine what was going on in his physical body at the time.

Please remember that it is not what you are doing, but where you are doing it. Here's why. Take a 12" wide plank and connect it to two buildings 5 feet off the ground and ask someone to walk across it. No problem. Now, take that same 12" wide plank up to the 30th floor and ask that same person to walk across it. I guarantee you will get a different response. It is not what you are doing, but where you are doing it.

What causes stress to manifest in the physical body besides walking on a 12" wide plank 30 stories high? Well, there is something that occurs while the Subconscious Mind is storing information, and it is responsible for causing stress in the physical body. This phenomenon creates what I refer to as Synthesizing Events.

Synthesizing Events

What we have learned up to this point is that the presence of stress in the physical body adversely affects us both physically and mentally. Physically, by weakening or switching off one or both sides of the physical body; and mentally, by weakening or switching off one or both hemispheres of the brain. When stress is present in the physical body, something is motivating the body to manifest stress. That something is a "synthesizing event."

A synthesizing event is created when the emotions from a traumatic experience actually synthesizes (comes together) with the information as it is being stored in the Subconscious Mind. This synthesized information remains stored and dormant in the Subconscious Mind until the Conscious Mind engages in some activity relative to the information. Once the Conscious Mind accesses this synthesized information it will manifest in the physical body as stress.

One of the best analogies I have ever heard in describing synthesizing events is to imagine that you have just purchased a brand new boat. The hull of this boat is clean and spotless. As time passes barnacles will attach themselves to the hull. The more barnacles that attach to the hull, the slower the boat will travel until the boat accumulates so many barnacles it stops all together.

Synthesizing events are like barnacles that have attached themselves to the hulls of our lives. If you accumulate enough barnacles they may manifest physically as a nervous breakdown or chronic illness, or mentally as sabotaging everything you do. The barnacle analogy is likened to mental baggage that your carry with you from game to game. When you accumulate too much mental baggage, the bottom falls out. What's responsible for creating synthesizing events? Trauma.

Webster's defines trauma as, "1. A bodily injury or shock; 2. An emotional shock, often having lasting psychic effects." As you can clearly see, trauma can be experienced both physically and mentally, and can range from mild to severe. The physical trauma from an automobile accident, for example, will heal with time. However, the mental (emotional) trauma may remain in the physical body for years unless you take some action to clear and release it. The intention of HK is to help players release trauma in the form of synthesizing events from their minds manifesting as stress in their physical bodies.

If you were ever at the plate with 2 outs in the bottom of the 9th with the winning run on 3rd base and struck out, you were traumatized. And, if you did it with 30,000 people watching you in the stands along with a television audience of about 20,000,000, it really traumatized you. Well, that experience created a synthesizing event which stored in your Subconscious Mind.

There are two types of synthesizing events. The "initial synthesizing event," and the "subsequent synthesizing event." The following analogy explains. Suppose you had a fear of heights. There was a first time you experienced that fear and it is referred to as the initial synthesizing event because it was the first time the synthesizing dynamics came into play relating to the experience.

That synthesized information is stored in your Subconscious Mind, and will remain dormant until you go near a high place again. Once this happens the

Conscious Mind sends instructions to the Subconscious Mind, "Send me all the information you have stored relating to being near a high place."

The stored information from the first experience comes up, and since an emotion has synthesized with the information, it surfaces as well. Your first reaction is, "Let's get away from this ledge!" The second experience created a subsequent synthesizing event.

Once you have left harm's way and are in a safe place, the initial synthesizing event is once again stored in your Subconscious Mind, and the subsequent synthesizing event is stored for the first time. Now you have two subconsciously stored pieces of information (or experiences) to support your fear of heights, and so on.

Let's revisit this bottom of the 9th scenario and assume you are in a situation where it's the bottom of the 9th, 2 outs, and the winning run is at 3rd base. You have a 3-2 count. The pitcher throws a pitch way outside the strike zone and you swing and miss; are called out on strikes; and your team loses the game.

That experience traumatized you and the next time you are in a similar situation, your Conscious Mind will send instructions to your Subconscious Mind, "Send me all the information you have stored relating to being in this situation." Since the information stored relating to the bottom of the 9th strike out was contaminated with a synthesizing event, it will create stress in your physical body and weakened or switched off one or both hemispheres of your brain.

In this weakened state, your performance will be marginal at best and may be the start of a hitting slump, and it may take weeks for you to recover. You will continue to repeat this pattern until the trauma responsible for contaminating your subconsciously store information relating to the experience is cleared.

Imagine an onion. Its center represents the kind of hitter you would like to become. Over the years you have accumulated layers of mental baggage (synthesizing events). This mental baggage is responsible for creating the problems you are now experiencing with your performance at the plate, and if you don't get rid of it you will carry it with you from game to game. In order to access the center of your onion (your true potential), the layers of mental baggage must be peeled away, and that is exactly what HK and this program will help you do.

It is my belief that 95% of all synthesizing events are stored in your Subconscious Mind during a period in your childhood development known as the Egocentric Stage.

The Egocentric Stage

There is a period in your childhood known as the egocentric stage, and it occurs between conception and 7 to 8 years of age. It was during this stage in your development when most of the synthesizing events were stored in your Subconscious Mind.

Webster's defines egocentricity as, "Regarding the self or the individual as the center of all things; Having little or no regard for interests or feelings other than one's own; Self-centered." The egocentric child is so self-centered that the first thought they have when something goes wrong in their lives is, "What did I do wrong?"

If you ask a three-year-old boy if he has a brother, he will answer yes. If you ask that same three-year-old boy if his brother has a brother, he will answer no. That's because the egocentric child cannot objectify his experience, he can only experience.

It's as if he cannot see himself. The reason for this phenomenon is that the egocentric child's Mind does not possess a critical factor. Remember that the critical factor allows your Mind to accept or reject incoming information passing through your Conscious Mind.

Without the capacity to criticize incoming information, the egocentric child's Subconscious Mind stores everything! At age 7 or 8 the child's critical factor starts kicking in. During the child's teen years, it is operating at full capacity because teenagers know everything and adults know nothing.

After the teen years, our criticalness starts reversing and by middle age, most of us experience a softening of our attitudes and come to realize that criticism was all a waste of good energy to begin with.

The absence of the critical factor also denies the egocentric child the capacity to rationalize. You cannot rationalize with someone who is incapable of objectifying his experiences. Some of the other anomalies associated with the egocentric child:

* Absolutize – You either love me or you hate me;
* Personalize - Takes everything personally;
* Idealize their role models – If dad says I'm stupid, it must be true;
* Self-blame – What did I do wrong;
* Shame – There must be something wrong with me;

Children have very limited resources when dealing with trauma. The only way they know how to deal with trauma is to block it out. They accomplish this by switching off one or both hemispheres of their brains depending on the severity of the trauma. This switching off will influence the decisions they make for the rest of their lives.

In the 1980's John Bradshaw brought to light much information relating to dysfunctional families. In a dysfunctional family, the members are simply not getting their needs met. But, what kind of a family environment would produce a functional child or adult? The following quote is from a book titled Trauma and Recovery by Dr. Judith Herman:

"The developing child's positive sense of self depends upon a caretaker's benign use of power. When a parent, who is so much more powerful than a child, nevertheless shows some regard for that child's individuality and dignity, that child feels

valued and respected; he develops self-esteem. He also develops autonomy, that is, a sense of his own separateness within a relationship. He learns to control and regulate his own bodily functions and to form and express his own point of view."

Wouldn't it have been nice to have been raised in this environment? The truth is that 99% of all families are dysfunctional. This dysfunction leaves most children who experience it filled with shame and doubt. Dr. Herman continues:

"Shame is a response to helplessness, the violation of bodily integrity, and the indignity suffered in the eyes of another person. Doubt reflects the inability to maintain one's own separate point of view while remaining in connection with others. In the aftermath of traumatic events, survivors doubt both others and themselves."

The switching off anomaly doesn't make children who experience it functional, it makes them <u>more</u> functional. Also, it is during this stage in our development that we accepted beliefs about ourselves that simply were not true. We accepted beliefs that we were not tall enough, thin enough, smart enough, this enough or that enough.

Here is an extraordinary example of how things we learn about ourselves during the egocentric stage of our development stay with us the rest of our lives. One day a teacher asked her students to list the names of the other students in the room on two sheets of paper, leaving a space between each name. Then she told them to think of the nicest thing they could say about each of their classmates and write it down. It took the remainder of the class period to finish their assignment, and as the students left the room, each one handed in the papers.

That Saturday, the teacher wrote down the name of each student on a separate sheet of paper, and listed what everyone else had said about that individual. On Monday she gave each student his or her list. Before long, the entire class was smiling. 'Really?' she heard whispered. "I never knew that I meant anything to anyone!" and, "I didn't know others liked me so much," were most of the comments.

No one ever mentioned those papers in class again. She never knew if the students discussed them after class or with their parents, but it didn't matter. The exercise had accomplished its purpose. The students were happy with themselves and one another. That group of students moved on.

Several years later, one of the students was killed in Viet Nam and his teacher attended the funeral of that special student. She had never seen a serviceman in a military coffin before. He looked so handsome, so mature. The church was packed with his friends. One by one those who loved him took a last walk by the coffin. The teacher was the last one to bless the coffin.

As she stood there, one of the soldiers who acted as pallbearer came up to her. "Were you Mark's math teacher?" he asked. She nodded, "Yes." Then he said, "Mark talked about you a lot." After the funeral, most of Mark's former classmates went together to a luncheon. Mark's mother and father were there, obviously waiting to speak with his teacher. "We want to show you something," his father said, taking a wallet out of his pocket. "They found this on Mark when he was killed. We thought you might recognize it."

Opening the billfold, he carefully removed two worn pieces of notebook paper that had obviously been taped, folded and refolded many times. The teacher knew without looking that the papers were the ones on which she had listed all the good things each of Mark's classmates had said about him. 'Thank you so much for doing that," Mark's mother said, "'As you can see, Mark treasured it."

All of Mark's former classmates started to gather around. Charlie smiled rather sheepishly and said, "I still have my list. It's in the top drawer of my desk at home." Chuck's wife said, "Chuck asked me to put his in our wedding album." "I have mine too," Marilyn said, "It's in my diary." Then Vicki, another classmate, reached into her pocketbook, took out her wallet and showed her worn and frazzled list to the group. "I carry this with me at all times," Vicki said and without batting an eyelash, she continued, "I think we all saved our lists."

If you tell a 6 year old he isn't good enough, he has no way of stopping that information. It goes right into subconscious storage and will be used at some point in his future to create his self-image. If you treat that same 6 years with respect and tell him he is loved and cherished he will, likewise, store the information subconsciously and it will have a profound positive impact on his self-image, and he will carry it with him for the rest of his life.

Many children start their baseball careers playing little league during the egocentric stage of their development. If you are a coach, please be ever mindful of what to tell these children whenever you interact with them. Because they respect you, they will believe everything you tell them.

If a child is shown respect, he learns to respect himself and others. Disrespecting a child traumatizes him. Sometimes the trauma is so severe that it causes both hemispheres of the brain to weaken or switch off. This creates a condition known as Dissociation.

Dissociation

As we had mentioned earlier, children do not have a lot of options when dealing with trauma. Children deal with it by blocking it out. They accomplish this by switching off one of both hemispheres of their brains depending upon the severity of the trauma. When both hemispheres of the brain switch off it creates a condition known as "dissociation."

Dissociation occurs when specific mental functions become separated (or dissociated) from the mainstream of consciousness and, as a consequence, are lost to the individual's awareness and voluntary control. When a batter, for instance, dissociates during an at bat, he cannot feel (Right Hemisphere switched off), nor is there structure to his swing or mental processes (Left Hemisphere switched off).

When your hemispheres are in this state, you'd might as well wear a blindfold when you take your at bat because your visit to the plate will not be very productive. There is a way to help you keep both hemispheres of your brain switched on during your visits to the plate. This is accomplished with the use of the HK Performance Trigger.

The HK Performance Trigger

We now know that when a batter experiences a traumatic encounter, the emotions from that trauma will synthesize with the information stored in his Subconscious Mind and adversely affect his future visits to the plate. In order to clear the synthesizing event, a desynthesis must occur. In order to reverse this phenomenon, I employ the HK Performance Trigger.

The HK Performance Trigger is used to release the trauma and all associated emotions connected to that trauma from your Subconscious Mind manifesting as stress in your physical body. In other words, the intention of the HK Performance Trigger is to sever the emotional trauma from the information stored in your Subconscious Mind creating the stress in your physical body. It works because "energy follows intention."

The more you do something the better you get at it. So, the more you use the HK Performance Trigger, the stronger and more effective it becomes. In HK, trauma, synthesizing events and mental baggage are all synonyms. The HK Performance Trigger was designed to help you peel away the psychological anomalies responsible for your problems at the plate.

This program utilizing the HK Performance Trigger is designed to help you perform to the best of your ability. The remainder of this book will show you how to program in the HK Performance Trigger, and how to use this program so that you may gain the maximum benefit.

Swing Mechanics

Earlier I had mentioned that when there is stress present in your body it will cause one or both hemispheres of your brain to weaken or switch off. This switching off phenomenon not only affects your thought processes during your at bats, but also will adversely affect your swing mechanics at the plate. Here's why.

The right hemisphere of your brain controls the left side of your physical body, while the left hemisphere of your brain controls the right side. When your right hemisphere weakens or switches off during the swing of your bat, it weakens the left side of your physical body. When you execute your swing at the plate, with a weak left side, it dramatically alters the mechanical dynamics of your swing.

When you swing at the plate with a weak left side, the mechanics of the batting stroke are seriously compromised. There is no way you can swing your bat with any consistency or accuracy with your body in this weakened state. This weakened state is so subtle it cannot be seen with the naked eye, and that is where muscle testing comes in.

During this weakened state your hand eye coordination and timing are severely compromised. With your swing mechanics in total chaos your visit to home plate will be a short one. The difference between the good hitters and the bad hitters is the 5" space between their ears.

This switching off phenomenon not only affects you physically, but mentally as well. For instance, when you are in your left hemisphere during your visit to the plate you will have a tendency to bat conservatively and not take any chances. You may often experience being called out on strikes. That's because the left hemisphere of your brain will plays it safe. Conversely, when your right hemisphere is dominating your thinking at the plate, you will have a tendency to strike out swinging. That's because your right hemisphere will take risks, while your left hemisphere will play it safe. You can see how this phenomenon will clearly affect the decisions you make at plate.

How many times have you seen a batter with 3-0 count, and winds up striking out. This book is designed to give you a resource. A resource to help you become as mentally prepared for your at bat as you can possibly become so that you may use that space between your ears to help you play your best to help your team win.

In HK, I employ the HK Performance Trigger to help you keep both hemispheres of your brain switched on during your visits to the plate. What you are about to learn in the following pages will help you remain calm, focused and relaxed during your at bats and help provide you with the mental clarity so that the decisions you make at the plate support you in doing your best to get on base or better.

Remaining calm, relaxed and focused allows your brain to function at maximum capacity. Since the brain controls all physical activity in the body, you will achieve peak performance while in this state.

Let's show you how to program in the HK Performance Trigger.

Programming In The HK Performance Trigger

There are three steps to programming in the HK Performance Trigger:

Step #1: Read the following statement aloud:

"I, (state your name), now accept and integrate into my Mind and body the HK Trigger which is stating, thinking or hearing the word 'relax' and touching the thumb and index fingers of both hands, to immediately and permanently neutralize all information manifesting as stress in every cell, organ and tissue of my physical body, and to 'switch on' the left and right hemispheres of my brain as well as my corpus callosum so that all three components function as one allowing me to always remain in present time, and to activate that part of my Mind that supports and allows me to experience and be open to receive more wealth, health, happiness, peace, joy, prosperity, safety and security in my life, and all other attributes I may require to help me experience the lifestyle of my choosing, to help me successfully accomplish all my goals, and to improve the quality of my life relating to every statement, thought and action I experience, layers one through infinity, and I will never interfere with the physical manifestation of all my goals, needs and desires, and every time I activate my HK Trigger it will become ten times more powerful, and to allow the HK Performance Trigger to help me always remain calm, relaxed, focused and productive during my at bats so that I may become a .400 plus hitter, and to help me do my best to help my team win every game in which I participate, and to help me clear all blockages preventing me from successfully accomplishing all my goals. This or something better."

<u>Step #2:</u> Say the word "relax" and touch the thumb and index fingers of both hands, then release and open your fingers.

<u>Step #3:</u> Read the statement in Step #1 again. Remember to read it aloud so that you involve as many of your senses as possible. The HK Performance Trigger, which is stating or thinking the word "relax" and touching the thumb and index fingers of both hands, is now programmed into your Subconscious Mind.

The HK Performance Trigger is intended to help you stay calm, relaxed and focused during your games, and most importantly during your visits to the plate because if you can remain relaxed when you execute your swing at the plate, both hemispheres of your brain will remain switched on. Physically it will help keep both sides of your body strong allowing the proper mechanical execution of your swing.

The HK Performance Trigger also provides you with the mental clarity necessary for you to make the best of your visit to the plate by providing you with a strategy that will support you in getting on base. This ultimately results in more consistent play and enhances your chances of making a positive contribution towards your team's efforts to win.

The HK Performance Trigger was designed to help you:

- To instantly, automatically and permanently release all trauma from every cell, organ and tissue manifesting as stress in your physical body;

- To instantly, automatically and permanently switch on and strengthen both hemispheres of your brain relating to every statement, thought or action you experience no matter what the activity;
- To stay calm, focused, relaxed and productive during your at bats;
- To do your best to win;
- To clear all blockages preventing you from successfully accomplishing all your goals.

There is an excellent process we use in Hemispheric Kinesiology to extract information from your Subconscious Mind. I call it HK Journaling.

HK Journaling

One of the limitations of the Conscious Mind is that it can only focus on one thing at a time. If you are having problems with your visits to the plate, there is usually more than one thing responsible for those problems. The HK Journaling exercise allows you to bring up those problems, or the negative experiences you had during your at bats, one at a time in order of their priority.

HK Journaling entails the use of open-ended statements to access subconsciously stored information manifesting as problems during your at bats. Grab a pencil and a blank piece of paper and draw a line down the center of the page. At the top of the left side of the page write the word Negative. At the top of the right side of the page write the word Positive.

Using open-ended statements list the negative things that occurred for you during your at bats on the left side of the page. For instance, let's assume that you have just finished a game where you had three at bats. Here is how you would document this information.

1. One of the negative things that occurred during my at bats was: I swung at several bad pitches;
2. The second negative thing that occurred during my at bats was: I kept getting behind in the count;
3. The third negative thing that occurred during my at bat was: Etc.

After you have finished documenting all the negative things that occurred for you during your at bats, go to the top of the right side of the page and document all the positive things that occurred for you during your at bats.

1. One of the positive things that occurred during my at bats was: I hit a double during my first at bat;
2. The second positive thing that occurred during my at bats was: I hit a sacrifice fly in the 7th inning which scored a run;
3. The third positive thing that occurred during my at bats was: Etc.

It is important to also focus on the positive things that occurred during your at bats because if you only focus on the negative that is all you will see. It reminds of an old saying I once heard, "You are never as good as you think you are, but you are never as bad either." Looking at both negative and positive elements of your visits to the plate just gives you a more balanced perspective on what's really going on for you.

As you can clearly see, the HK Journaling exercise allows you to document a tremendous amount of information regarding your at bats, and the problems that came up for you. Now, let's discuss how the HK Performance Trigger is used to clear the information that surfaced for you during your post game evaluation.

How To Use The HK Performance Trigger

With the onion analogy I explained that the center of the onion represents the type of power hitter you have the potential to become. Over the years you have accumulated layers of mental baggage in the form of synthesizing events that are responsible for preventing you from becoming that player. What's creating problems with your at bats right now is the fact that you carry this mental baggage with from one at bat to the next. It's as if you are walking through a mental revolving door.

I suggest that you do the HK Journaling exercise after each and every game in which you have an at bat. What follows is a four step process that will allow you to peel away the layers of mental baggage responsible for creating the problems you are now experiencing with your hitting:

Step #1: If you haven't already, go back to the chapter on Programming In The HK Performance Trigger. Program in the trigger by following Steps 1 through 3 (Once the trigger is programmed in you never have to do it again);

Step #2: Read your HK Journaling list starting with the negative things that came up for you during your at bats, and read them one at a time;

Step #3: After reading the first item on the negative side of your list, hit your trigger. Say or mentally state the word "relax" and touch the thumb and index fingers of both your hands, and open them. Move to the second negative thing and do the same thing until you have gone through the entire negative list;

<u>Step #4:</u> Now, move to the positive list and repeat Step #3 until you have gone through the entire positive list;

Here's why this is so effective. Suppose that one of the negative things that came up for you was that you swung at several bad pitches. When you read this sentence, your Conscious Mind will send instructions to your Subconscious Mind, "Send me all the stored information you have relating to why I swung at several bad pitches."

When that information surfaces, it will no doubt have a synthesizing event connected to it. When you hit your HK Performance Trigger it will neutralize whatever created the stress, and will allow you to peel another layer from this onion that has grown around your hitting. The more layers you can peel off, the closer you will get to the center.

My suggestion is to punch holes in the completed forms and keep them in a three ring binder. Once a month or so, review them and see if you can find any patterns that may be developing with your at bats that need addressing. In fact, the question you should be asking yourself after each failed at bat is, "What could I have done to have gotten a hit or better during my last at bat?"

If you don't think this post performance evaluation process is effective, Byron Nelson, a former PGA Tour player, won 18 tournaments in one year back in the 1940's (11 in a row!) doing the exact same thing. If it worked for him, it will certainly work for you.

The HK Performance Trigger can also be used during batting practice and during your at bats in actual game conditions as a Pre-Swing Routine.

The Pre-Swing Routine

You will be integrating this pre-swing routine into your at bats for one reason and one reason only, to help you become as calm and relaxed as possible during the execution of your swing! When you are relaxed during your at bats, it allows you to keep both hemispheres of your brain switched on which keeps both sides of your physical body strong allowing you to mechanically execute your swing so that you dramatically increase your chances of getting a hit or better.

Here's how you do the pre-swing routine before a pitch:

1. Before you step into the batter's box, mentally state your goal for your at bat (i.e., my goal is to get a base hit or better during this at bat);
2. Mentally state the word "relax" and step into the batter's box and prepare yourself to receive the next pitch;

Now, let's assume that you are at the plate and took a swing at the first pitch and missed. The first thing you must understand is that your body never does anything arbitrarily. If you swing and miss, something motivated your body to swing and miss. That something is mental baggage in the form of a synthesizing event which surfaced in your body from your Subconscious Mind and subsequently manifested as stress. You swung and missed because there was stress present in your body.

After your swing and miss, step away from the plate and ask yourself, "Why did I swing and miss?" Then hit your trigger by mentally stating the word "relax." This question causes your Conscious Mind to send instructions to your Subconscious Mind, i.e., "Send me all the information you have stored relating to why I swung and missed that last pitch." This procedure allows you to peel away any layers of whatever caused you to swing and miss. It also insures that you won't carry that disappointment, or any other emotional reaction, with you into your next swing.

There are many reasons why this pre-swing routine is so effective. The most important reason is that it allows you to remain calm, relaxed and focused on your whole purpose for being at the plate, and that is to get a hit or better. It also allows you to set a goal for each at bat, and the continued use of the HK Performance Trigger will help you stay relaxed resulting in a more productive at bat.

Another excellent advantage in using this pre-swing routine is a phenomenon known as "compounding." Compounding occurs when the same suggestion is layered upon itself many times. The incessant use of the word relax will eventually condition your body to remain relaxed during your visits to the plate and that is when you achieve peak performance. Your hitting will become much more consistent, and you may even begin to enjoy the experience.

Mind Mastery For Hitting

I have created a program for hitters call *Mind Mastery For Hitting*. It includes a DVD and a CD. The DVD is titled *Change Your Thinking, Change Your Life*. The DVD explains HK and how I use muscle testing during my sessions.

The CD is titled *Becoming A 400 Hitter.* At the beginning of the CD I have programmed in the same HK Performance Trigger (relax) contained in this book. The CD, for instance, contains over 100 statements relating to hitting and wining. Each statement is followed by the trigger word "relax."

Listening to the CD before your game allows you to become as mentally prepared for your at bats as possible. Listening to the CD after your game helps to peel away layers of mental baggage that came up for you during your visits to the plate that day. If you are not hitting to the best of your ability, it simply means that your "stuff" (mental baggage) came up during your at bats. This stuff, in the form of synthesizing events, is responsible for the problems you are experiencing in your performances at the plate.

If you have been playing baseball for 10 years, you have 10 years worth of information stored in your Subconscious Mind relating to hitting. If some of that information was contaminated with synthesizing events, it was put there in layers over this 10 year period. Listening to the CD helps to peel away these layers and puts you on the road to becoming the kind of hitter you would like to become. It literally changes the subconsciously stored information you have accumulated over the years relating to your hitting.

When you are out there standing in the batter's box, your Conscious Mind will send instructions to your

Subconscious Mind, "Send me all the information you have in storage relating to hitting." If part of the information you access that day is creating stress in your physical body (synthesizing events), you will not be very productive during your visit to the batter's box.

The layers of mental blockages must be removed in layers because that's the way they were stored. Listening to the CD that evening after each game will allow you to clear whatever stuff came up for you earlier that day. If you experience a really horrible outing at the plate, that's when you really need to listen to the CD. As I mentioned earlier, it simply means that your stuff was up. Please do your best to remain object.

I recommend that you listen to the *Becoming A .400 Hitter* CD every day for the first 30 days. After 30 days, listen to the CD one to two hours before game time, and the evening after every game. This allows you to clear any synthesizing events that came up for you during your at bats that day so that you don't carry them with you into your next game.

One to two hours before game time find a quiet location and sit or recline so that you are comfortable. Do your best to listen to each statement. If you take a deep breath or yawn after a statement, it simply means that you have cleared something on a subconscious level relating to one of the statements you heard while listing to the CD.

Sometimes it is difficult for you to take 30 minutes out of your day to sit down and listen to a CD. I suggest that you buy a small portable CD player and place it on the headboard of you bed. Turn it on before you drift off to sleep with the volume low. It is recommended that you listen to the CD while conscious and awake. However, you will still derive substantial benefits listening to the CD as you drift off to sleep. You may also listen to the CD in your car on the way to the game.

I cannot adequately stress the significance of listening to the CD every day you touch a bat. Even when you take batting practice you are accessing information from your Subconscious Mind relating to hitting. Some of the information you access during your practice sessions will have synthesizing events attached to them, and they must be cleared or you will carry them with you into your next game. Listening to the CD helps you to accomplish this.

Setting Goals

After Tiger Woods won his first Masters, he skipped a tournament, and came back and won the next tournament. During his post tournament interview, he was asked why he thought he won the tournament. Tiger looked at the interviewer with surprise and replied, "Because it was my goal to win it."

How does your physical body know what your mind expects from it if you do not set a goal? Set a goal for each game and at bat. Even if your body sabotages your efforts when you set a goal, at least give it the benefit of the doubt. ALWAYS SET A GOAL!!!

You are setting a goal for each at bat when you use your pre-swing routine. Here's what you do to set a goal for each game. The night before the game, grab a pencil and paper and write your goal. Read your goal aloud, and hit your trigger.

Example:

Step #1: I, <u>player's name</u>, will do my best to help my team _____ win the game today/tonight against _____, and I will do my best to secure a hit or better during all my at bats. I will remain calm, relaxed and focused and help my team win the game, and I will never interfere with the physical manifestation of this goal, this or something better;

Step #2: Hit your HK Performance Trigger by stating or thinking the word "relax" and touching the thumb and index fingers of both hands, and opening them;

Step #3: Read your goal aloud again.

I suggest that you set goals at the beginning of the season. For instance, what would you like your batting average to be at the end of the season? How many RBIs would you like to record? Would you like to be selected as an all star that year? Write these goals down, read and clear each one of them every day using your HK Trigger.

Anytime you do something different your body sends up a red flag and says something like, "Wait a minute, no body sent me a memo, what are you doing?" If you are not accustomed to setting goals, the first several times you do it your body may ignore or sabotage your efforts. Do your best to remain objective and ALWAYS SET A GOAL BEFORE EACH SEASON, AT BAT AND BEFORE EACH GAME!

Using Your Imagination During Batting Practice

Imagination is defined as, "The action or faculty of forming mental images or concepts of what is not actually present to the senses." When you imagine yourself doing something, you are going to subconsciously access the same information as if you were physically doing it. Using your imagination during batting practice has a twofold benefit.

First, since your imagination is located in the right hemisphere of your brain, every time you use it you are exercising that part of your brain. If you can keep your the right hemisphere of your brain switched on during practice, chances are you will keep it switched on during your games.

Secondly, your Subconscious Mind cannot distinguish between something real or imagined. Using imagination in conjunction with the HK Performance Trigger allows you to clear any synthesizing events you may have stored relating to a particular batting situation.

Think of the most stressful situation you normally encounter during your visits to the plate, and mentally imagine yourself in that situation during batting practice. For instance, imagine that you are facing the best pitcher in the league, and it's the bottom of the ninth, bases loaded, two outs, and the winning run is on second base. If you have problems hitting the next pitch, chances you will have problems hitting that pitch in an actual situation. Ask yourself why you had problems hitting that pitch.

Then hit your HK Performance Trigger by mentally stating or thinking the word "relax." Keep creating that situation until you are satisfied with your swing. Then move on to other stressful situations you encounter during your games and repeat the same procedure. What's very helpful in clearing out past problems you may have had at the plate is to imagine yourself in that same situation, and see if you can execute a good swing. If you can't, hit your trigger and do it again until you are satisfied with your swing.

Even though the ball is not coming at 95 miles per hour this exercise is still very affective because your Subconscious Mind cannot distinguish between something real or imagined.

Imagination is so effective that before the final round of the 1994 United States Women's Open Golf Championships, Lauri Merten was on the practice putting green imagining herself putting to win the tournament. Four hours later she was hoisting the trophy as the 1994 United States Women's Golf Open champion. Imagination is a very powerful and effective tool, and it works. I entreat you to religiously integrate it into your practice regime.

Conclusion

In 2000, a gentleman from North Carolina purchased a Mind Mastery For Hitting program from me for his son. A year later he sent me this e-mail:

"My son first began using the Mind Mastery For Hitting program at the end of his junior year in high school. The season that followed was just remarkable. The change in focus and concentration made a big difference in his approach not only to hitting, but on the ball field as well. He carried this success to fall ball and was selected to play on a showcase travel team that played at all the major colleges and universities in our area.

He played every weekend in front of college and pro scouts. At the end...he had eight colleges to choose from to play at the next level. During his tryout at the college he had eventually chosen, he went 3 for 3 at the plate. I can say that the Mind Mastery For Hitting program is the one key that made the difference. His hitting fundamentals were constant and remained the same. Thanks for such a great program. I would highly recommend this program to anybody interested in improving their game."

I am not sharing this to brag, but to simple state that if you follow this program you will see a dramatic improvement in your hitting. I don't know what you will have to do to become the kind of hitter you would like to become, but on some level of your awareness you do.

Doing the HK program faithfully will allow you to peel away the layers of synthesizing events you have accumulated over the years responsible for preventing you from realizing your true potential as a power hitter.

To gain the maximum benefit from *Mastering The Mental Side Of Hitting* it is important to use the entire program which entails:

- Programming in the HK Performance Trigger;
- Using your HK Performance Trigger along with your imagination during batting practice;
- Using your pre-swing routine before each swing;
- Setting goals before each season, game and at bat;
- Faithfully doing your post game evaluations using the HK Journaling exercise;
- Religiously listening to the CD *Becoming A 400 Hitter.*

It is said that adversity introduces a man to himself. I trust that the next time you encounter adversity in the batter's box that you will remain objective enough to understand where it came from and how to constructively remedy it. Remember, that baseball, like life, is relative, and that among the blind, the one eyed man is King. "Relax"

****

Other HK products available at www.hk-relax.com and
amazon.com:

Mind Mastery For Golf
Mind Mastery For Soccer
Mind Mastery For Tennis
Mind Mastery For Hitting
Mind Mastery For Football
Mind Mastery For Pitching
Mind Mastery For Coaching
Mind Mastery For Basketball
Mind Mastery For Winning
Mind Mastery For Money
Mind Mastery For Selling
Mind Mastery For Peace Of Mind
Mind Mastery For Learning
Mind Mastery For Weight Loss
Change Your Thinking Change Your Life (DVD)

Other books by Ernest Solivan available at lulu.com and
amazon.com:

When The Wheels Fly Off
Mastering The Mental Side Of Soccer
Mastering The Mental Side Of Tennis
Mastering The Mental Side Of Hitting
Mastering The Mental Side Of Football
Mastering The Mental Side Of Pitching
Mastering The Mental Side Of Coaching
Mastering The Mental Side Of Basketball
Mastering The Mental Side Of Winning
Mastering The Mental Side Of Putting
Quantum Psychophysics
Pro Se Cites & Authorities

For more information about Hemispheric
Kinesiology contact:
Performance Consultants International
Website: www.hk-relax.com

www.ingramcontent.com/pod-product-compliance
Lightning Source LLC
LaVergne TN
LVHW091201080426
835509LV00006B/771